Saunders $16.85
(jnf)

P9-DFR-567

MIGHTY MACHINES

Bulldozers

by M. T. Martin

BELLWETHER MEDIA · MINNEAPOLIS, MN

Note to Librarians, Teachers, and Parents:

Blastoff! Readers are carefully developed by literacy experts and combine standards-based content with developmentally appropriate text.

Level 1 provides the most support through repetition of high-frequency words, light text, predictable sentence patterns, and strong visual support.

Level 2 offers early readers a bit more challenge through varied simple sentences, increased text load, and less repetition of high-frequency words.

Level 3 advances early-fluent readers toward fluency through increased text and concept load, less reliance on visuals, longer sentences, and more literary language.

Whichever book is right for your reader, Blastoff! Readers are the perfect books to build confidence and encourage a love of reading that will last a lifetime!

This edition first published in 2007 by Bellwether Media.

No part of this publication may be reproduced in whole or in part without written permission of the publisher. For information regarding permission, write to Bellwether Media Inc., Attention: Permissions Department, Post Office Box 1C, Minnetonka, MN 55345-9998.

Library of Congress Cataloging-in-Publication Data
Martin, M. T. (Martin Theodore)
  Bulldozers / by M. T. Martin.
    p. cm. — (Blastoff! readers) (Mighty machines)
Summary: "Simple text and supportive images introduce young readers to bulldozers. Intended for students in kindergarten through third grade."
  Includes bibliographical references and index.
  ISBN-10: 1-60014-043-2 (hardcover : alk. paper)
  ISBN-13: 978-1-60014-043-3 (hardcover : alk. paper)
  1. Bulldozers—Juvenile literature. 2. Earthwork—Juvenile literature. I. Title. II. Series. III. Series: Mighty machines (Bellwether Media)

TA725.M335 2006
624.1'52—dc22   2006007211

Text copyright © 2007 by Bellwether Media.
Printed in the United States of America.

Table of Contents

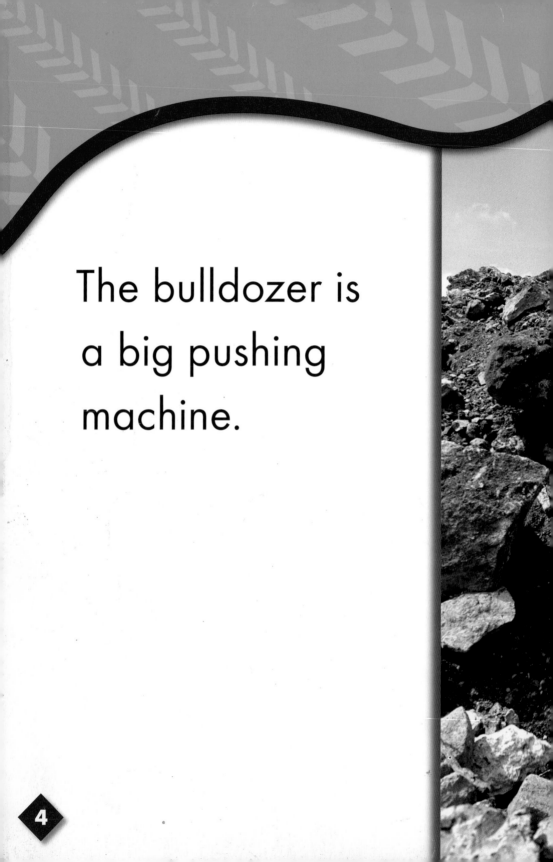

The bulldozer is
a big pushing
machine.

The bulldozer has a **cab**. A worker sits in the cab.

cab

The bulldozer has **tracks**.

tracks

The tracks
can travel over
sand and mud.

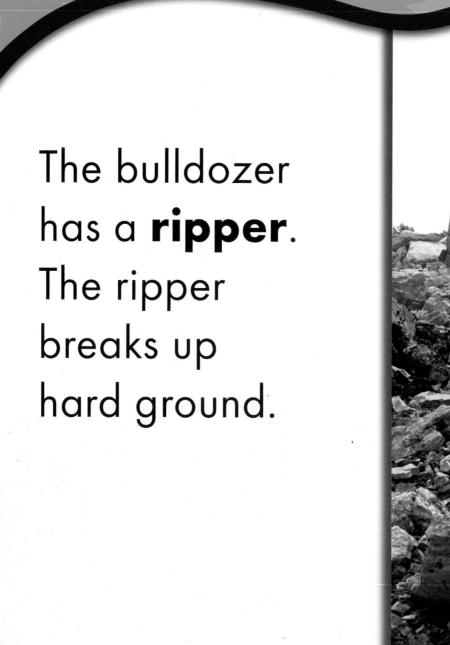

The bulldozer has a **ripper**. The ripper breaks up hard ground.

ripper

The bulldozer has a strong **blade**. The blade can be as heavy as an elephant.

blade

The blade
pushes dirt.

This bulldozer flattens the ground. It makes a new yard.

This bulldozer
works at
a race track.
The bulldozer is
a great machine.

Glossary

blade—a large piece of flat metal at the front of a bulldozer

cab—the place where a worker sits

ripper—strong metal spikes that tear apart hard ground

tracks—a metal band that bulldozers use instead of wheels

To Learn More

AT THE LIBRARY

Glover, David and Penny. *Bulldozers*. North Mankato, Minn.: Smart Apple Media, 2005.

Jones, Melanie Davis. *Big Machines*. New York: Children's Press, 2002.

Sargent, Sam. *Bulldozers*. Osceola, Wis.: Motorbooks International, 1994.

ON THE WEB

Learning more about mighty machines is as easy as 1, 2, 3.

1. Go to www.factsurfer.com

2. Enter "mighty machines" into search box.

3. Click the "Surf" button and you will see a list of related web sites.

With factsurfer.com, finding more information is just a click away.

Index